This Day the LORD has Made

A Christian Easter Coloring Book

Synthography by B. Marie Kirkland

In the beginning was the Word, and the Word was with God, and the Word was God.

John 1:1

...the angel Gabriel was sent from God to a virgin who's name was Mary.

And the angel said unto her, Fear not, for thou hast found favour with God, thou shalt conceive in thy womb, and bring forth a son, and shalt call his name Jesus...

And of his kingdom there shall be no end.

For with God nothing shall be impossible.

Luke 1:26-37

And she brought forth her firstborn son, and wrapped him in swaddling clothes, and laid him in a manger; because there was no room for them in the inn.

Luke 2:7

and, lo, the star, which they saw in the east, went before them, till it came and stood over where the young child was.

Matthew 2:9

And all they that heard it wondered at those things which were told them by the shepherds concerning the child.

But Mary kept all these things, and pondered them in her heart.

Luke 2:18-19

The Holy Spirit was upon Simeon and when he saw the Christ child, he said:

"Sovereign Lord, as you have promised, you may now dismiss your servant in peace.
For my eyes have seen your salvation, which you have prepared in the sight of all nations: a light for revelation to the Gentiles, and the glory of your people Israel."

And the child's father and mother marveled at what was said about him.

Luke 2:25-33

And the child grew and became strong; he was filled with wisdom, and the grace of God was on him.

Luke 2:40

And when he was twelve years old, they went up to Jerusalem after the custom of the feast.

as they returned, the child Jesus tarried behind in Jerusalem; and Joseph and his mother knew not of it.

after three days they found him in the temple
And all that heard him were astonished at his understanding and answers.

he returned with his parents to Nazareth and did their bidding
but his mother kept all these sayings in her heart.

And Jesus increased in wisdom and stature, and in favour with God and man.

Luke 2:42-52

"...And she treasured them in her heart..."

Mary's faith ran deep and strong,
guarding the secrets of God and gracefully
awaiting their fulfillment.

The voice of one crying in the wilderness:
Prepare ye the way of the Lord, make his
paths straight.
And all flesh shall see the salvation of
God.

John said unto them all:
I indeed baptize you with water; but one
mightier than I cometh, the latches of
whose shoes I am not worthy to unloose:

he shall baptize you with the Holy Ghost
and with fire:

Luke 3:4-6

And it came to pass in those days, that Jesus came from Nazareth of Galilee, and was baptized of John in Jordan.

And straightway coming up out of the water, he saw the heavens opened, and the Spirit like a dove descending upon him

And there came a voice from heaven, saying, Thou art my beloved Son, in whom I am well pleased.

Mark 1:9-11

And Jesus being full of the Holy Ghost was led by the Spirit into the wilderness,
Being forty days tempted of the devil.

And the devil took him to a high mountain, showing him all the kingdoms of the world in a moment of time.
The devil said unto him, all this power will I give thee... If you will worship me...

And Jesus answered and said unto him, Get thee behind me, Satan: for it is written, Thou shalt worship the Lord thy God, and him only shalt thou serve.

Luke 4:5-8

And he came to Nazareth, where he had been brought up: and in the synagogue proclaimed that he was the Messiah.

And they said, Is not this Joseph's son?
And he said, Verily I say unto you:
No prophet is accepted in his own country.
And would not perform miracles.

they were filled with wrath, rose up and took him to a cliff to cast him off of it.

But he passing through the midst of them went his way unseen.

Luke 4:16-30

And it came to pass, that, as the people pressed upon him to hear the word of God, he stood by the lake of Gennesaret,

And saw two ships standing by the lake: but the fishermen were gone out of them, and were washing their nets.

Luke 5:1-2

Now when he had left speaking, he said unto Simon, Launch out into the deep, and let down your nets for a catch.

And Simon said unto him, Master, we have toiled all the night, and have taken nothing: nevertheless at thy word I will let down the net.

And when they had this done, they enclosed a great multitude of fishes. And he was astonished, and all that were with him, at the draught of the fishes which they had taken.

Luke 5:4-5

Then Jesus said to Simon, "Don't be afraid; from now on you will be fishers of men."

So they pulled their boats up on shore, left everything and followed him.

Luke 5:10-11

But their scribes and Pharisees murmured against his disciples, saying, Why do ye eat and drink with tax collectors and sinners?

And Jesus answering said unto them, They that are whole need not a physician; but they that are sick.

I came not to call the righteous, but sinners to repentance.

Luke 5:30-32

And it came to pass in those days that He went out onto a mountain to pray, and continued all night in prayer to God.

And when it was day, He called unto Him His disciples, and from them He chose twelve, whom also He named apostles.

Luke 6:12-13

Shortly before dawn Jesus went out to his Apostles in the boat, walking on the lake.

When the disciples saw him walking on the water, they were terrified. "It's a ghost," they said, and cried out in fear.

But Jesus immediately said to them: "Take courage! It is I. Do not be afraid."

Matthew 14:22-27

Jesus took Peter, John and James with him and went up onto a mountain to pray.

As he was praying, the appearance of his face changed, and his clothes became as bright as a flash of lightning. Two men, Moses and Elijah, appeared in glorious splendor, talking with Jesus.

While he was speaking, a cloud appeared and covered them, and a voice came from the cloud, saying, "This is my Son, whom I have chosen; listen to him."

Luke 9:28-36

God's Kingdom is like a mustard seed that, when sown upon the soil, is the smallest of all the seeds on the ground.

And when sown, it comes up and grows taller than all the garden plants, and produces large branches, so that the birds of the sky can nest in its shade.

Mark 4:31

Jesus said,

"What do you think? If a man owns a hundred sheep, and one of them wanders away, will he not leave the ninety-nine on the hills and go to look for the one that wandered off?

And if he finds it, truly I tell you, he is happier about that one sheep than about the ninety-nine that did not wander off. In the same way your Father in heaven is not willing that any of these little kids should perish."

Matthew 18:12-14

Jesus said, "Let the little children come to me, and do not hinder them, for the kingdom of heaven belongs to such as these."

Matthew 19:14

Then Satan entered Judas Iscariot, one of the Twelve.

And Judas went to the chief priests and the officers of the temple guard and discussed with them how he might betray Jesus.

They were delighted and agreed to give him money.

He consented, and watched for an opportunity to hand Jesus over to them when no crowd was present.

Luke 22:3-6

And he took bread, gave thanks and broke it, and gave it to them, saying, "This is my body given for you; do this in remembrance of me."

In the same way, after the supper he took the cup, saying, "This cup is the new covenant in my blood, which is poured out for you."

Luke 22:19-20

He took Peter, James and John along with him in the Garden of Gethsemane to pray, and he began to be deeply distressed and troubled.

"My soul is overwhelmed with sorrow to the point of death," he said to them.

Going a little farther, he fell to the ground and prayed that if possible the hour might pass from him. "Abba, Father," he said, "everything is possible for you. Take this cup from me. Yet not what I will, but what you will."

Mark 14:33-36

Judas led armed men to the Garden of Gethsemane where he knew Jesus would be praying with his disciples and no others would be near to stop Jesus's arrest.

Mark 14:43

Now the betrayer had arranged a signal with them: "The one I kiss is the man; arrest him and lead him away under guard."
Going at once to Jesus, Judas said, "Rabbi!" and kissed him.

The men seized Jesus and arrested him.

Mark 14:44-46

Jesus asked him, "Judas, are you betraying the Son of Man with a kiss?"

Luke 22:48

His disciples said, "Lord, should we strike with our swords?"

And one of them struck the servant of the high priest, cutting off his right ear. But Jesus answered, "No more of this!" And he touched the man's ear and healed him.

Then Jesus said to the mob, "Am I leading a rebellion, that you have come with swords and clubs? Every day I was with you in the temple courts, and you did not lay a hand on me.

But this is your hour—when darkness reigns."

Luke 22:48

Pilate called together the people and said: "I have examined him have found no basis for your charges against him. I will punish and release him."

But the whole crowd shouted, "Away with this man! Release the murderer Barrabas to us!"

Pilate appealed to them twice more, but they kept shouting, "Crucify him! Crucify him!"

So Pilate granted their demand and surrendered Jesus to their will.

Luke 23:13-25

When they came to the place called the Hill of Golgotha (Skull), they crucified him there, along with the criminals—one on his right, the other on his left.

Jesus said, "Father, forgive them, for they do not know what they are doing.

It was now about noon, and darkness came over the whole land until three in the afternoon, for the sun stopped shining. And the curtain of the temple was torn in two by an earthquake.

Luke 23:33-45

Near the cross of Jesus stood his mother, his mother's sister, Mary the wife of Clopas, and Mary Magdalene.

When Jesus saw his mother there, and the disciple whom he loved standing nearby, he said to her, "Woman, here is your son," and to the disciple, "Here is your mother."

From that time on, this disciple took her into his home.

John 19:25-27

Jesus called out with a loud voice:

"Father, into your hands I commit my spirit."

When he had said this, he breathed his last.

All those who knew him, including the women who had followed him from Galilee, stood at a distance, watching these things.

Luke 23:46-49

Now there was a man named Joseph, a member of the Council, a good and upright man, who had not consented to their decision and action. He came from the Judean town of Arimathea, and he himself was waiting for the kingdom of God.

Going to Pilate, he asked for Jesus' body. Then he took it down, wrapped it in linen cloth and placed it in a tomb cut in the rock, one in which no one had yet been laid.

Then he rolled a stone against the entrance of the tomb.

Luke 23:50-53
Mark 15:42-46

On the first day of the week, very early in the morning, the women took the spices they had prepared and went to the tomb.

They found the stone rolled away from the tomb, but could not find the body of the Lord Jesus.

Suddenly two men in clothes that gleamed like lightning stood beside them. The men said to them, "Why do you look for the living among the dead?

He *is* not here; he has risen!

Luke 24:1-6

Now Mary stood outside the tomb crying. There was a man there who she assumed was the gardener.

He asked her, "Woman, why are you crying? Who is it you are looking for?" "Sir, my Lord is missing and if you have carried him away, tell me where you have put him, and I will get him," she said.

Jesus said to her, "Mary." She turned toward him and cried out in Aramaic, "Teacher!"

John 20:11-16

Later, Jesus appeared to his disciples, to their astonishment. He reminded them that he had fulfilled the Law and the Prophets.

Then he opened their minds so they could understand the Scriptures.

After the Lord Jesus had spoken to them, he was taken up into heaven and he sat at the right hand of God.

Then the disciples went out and preached everywhere, and the Lord worked with them and confirmed his word by the signs that accompanied it.

Mark 16 and Luke 24

The Promise of Easter

This is the Day the Lord has made, let us rejoice and be glad in it.

Psalm 118:24

"Even on the cross He *did not hide Himself from sight; rather, He made all creation witness to the presence of its Maker.*"

— St. Athanasius

"Be not anxious about what you have, but about what you are."
— St. Gregory the Great

"One thing there is that is not beneath the dignity of God, and that is, to do good to him that needed it."
— Gregory of Nyssa

I *am the good shepherd. The good shepherd gives His life for the sheep.*

But *a hireling, he who is not the shepherd, one who does not own the sheep, sees the wolf coming and leaves the sheep and flees; and the wolf catches the sheep and scatters them.*

The *hireling flees because he is a hireling and does not care about the sheep.*

I *am the good shepherd; and I know My sheep, and am known by My sheep.*

John 10:11-15

"For *no part of Creation is left void of him:*
he has filled all things everywhere."

— St. Athanasius

No one is truly poor but except the one who lacks the truth.

— Ephrem the Syrian

As the deer pants for streams of water,
so my soul pants for you, my God.

Psalm 42:1

Commit your activities to the Lord, and your plans will be established.

Proverbs 16:3

My son, do not despise the Lord's discipline,
and do not resent his rebuke,
because the Lord disciplines those he loves,
as a father the son he delights in.

Proverbs 3:11

For with you is the fountain of life; in your light we see light.

Psalm 36:9

"I *am sending you out like sheep among wolves. Therefore be as shrewd as snakes and as innocent as doves.*"

Matthew 10:16

Jesus said,

"You are the light of the world.
A town built on a hill cannot be hidden.

Neither do people light a lamp and put it under a bowl. Instead they put it on its stand, and it gives light to everyone in the house.

In the same way, let your light shine before others, that they may see your good deeds and glorify your Father in heaven."

Matthew 5:14-16

Flee from youthful lusts and follow righteousness, faith, charity, peace with them that call on the Lord out of a pure heart.

Timothy 2:22

Even though I walk
through the darkest valley,
I will fear no evil,
for you are with me.

Psalm 23:4

O Lord, how manifold are your works! In wisdom have you made them all; the earth is full of your creatures. Here is the sea, great and wide, which teems with creatures innumerable, living things both small and great.

Psalm 104:24-25

He *makes springs pour water into the ravines;*
it flows between the mountains.

They *give water to all the beasts of the field;*
the wild donkeys quench their thirst.
The birds of the sky nest by the waters; they
sing among the branches.

He *makes grass grow for the cattle,*
and plants for people to cultivate—bringing
forth food from the earth:

wine that gladdens human hearts,
oil to make their faces shine,
and bread that sustains their hearts.

Psalms 104:10-15

Do not store up for yourselves treasures on earth, where moths and vermin destroy, and where thieves break in and steal.

But store up for yourselves treasures in heaven.

For where your treasure is, there your heart will be also.

Matthew 6:19-21

Jesus said, "I am the vine; you are the branches. If you remain in me and I in you, you will bear much fruit; apart from me you can do nothing.

My command is this: Love each other as I have loved you."

John 15:5

For his anger lasts only a moment, but his favor lasts a lifetime; weeping may stay for the night, but rejoicing comes in the morning.

Psalm 30:5

Jesus said,

"how often I have longed to gather my children together, as a hen gathers her chicks under her wings..."

Matthew 23:37

But let all who take refuge in you be glad; let them ever sing for joy. Spread your protection over them, that those who love your name may rejoice in you.

Psalm 5:11

Get rid of the old yeast, so that you may be a new unleavened batch— sinless as you really are.

For Christ, our Passover lamb, has been sacrificed for us.

Corinthians 5:7

"This, then, is how you should pray:

Our Father in heaven,
hallowed be your name,
10 your kingdom come,
your will be done,
on earth as it is in heaven.
Give us today our daily bread.
And forgive us our debts,
as we also have forgiven our debtors.
And lead us not into temptation,
but deliver us from the evil one."

Matthew 6:9-13

Test your colors here!

Made in the USA
Las Vegas, NV
27 March 2024

87776849R00070